I0558963

In Memory of Peanut the Squirrel and Fred the Raccoon

A Tribute to Two Heroes and the Lives They Changed

Willow Hart

In Memory of Peanut the Squirrel and Fred the Racoon
Copyright 2024. Willow Hart

All Rights Reserved
No part of this book may be reproduced in any manner
without the author's written consent except in the case of
brief excerpts in critical reviews and articles.

Inquiries about this book should
be addressed to the Publisher:
Email: sutterhouse2010@gmail.com

Printed in the USA

ISBN: 979-8-9921146-0-7 (paperback
979-8-9921146-1-4 (ebook)

As part of the passion was the Author's personal experience in watching what happened to this animal rescue and the insane, barbaric actions of the government. I, like you, were moved by this story and the reason for this book. To bring hope to those equally affected and to put a little sunshine where darkness had reared its ugly head. Proceeds from this writing will go to *P'nuts Freedom Farm Animal Sanctuary* to assist the Sanctuary with needed funds in fighting and suing the government and whatever they need to use the money for to survive.

Please contact:
P'nuts Freedom Farm Animal Sanctuary Inc.
TAX ID: 93-2182780

https://www.pnutsfreedomfarm.com/

https://www.paypal.com/donate/?cmd=_don
ations&business=pnutsfreedomfarm@gmail.
com&item_name=P%E2%80%99Nuts%20
Freedom%20Farm%20Animal%20
Sanctuary&currency_code=USD

Chapter 1:
Peanut the Hero

The house was alive with the sounds of life.

A soft hum of voices spilled from the kitchen, where Claudia, a German transplant to New York State and wife was mixing bottles of formula for two orphaned baby opossums. The rhythmic clatter of a raccoon rummaging through a cabinet echoed from the next room, followed by a triumphant grunt and the unmistakable *pop* of a peanut butter jar being opened.

"Fred!" she called, her voice half-scolding, half-amused. "That's the third jar this week!"

"Hey, it's not my fault the good stuff's on the top shelf," Fred replied, waddling into the room with the jar clutched in his paws.

The lady sighed but smiled, shaking her head. "You're lucky you're cute."

On the back of the couch, perched like a tiny king on his throne, Peanut twitched his tail. His bright, curious eyes followed Fred's every move as the raccoon climbed onto a chair and proceeded to smear peanut butter all over his face.

"You're disgusting," Peanut said, his voice full of mock anger.

Fred didn't miss a beat. "And you're boring." He licked a glob of peanut butter off his paw. "When's the last time you did anything fun?"

1

"Fun?" Peanut tilted his head, his nose twitching. "I'm the face of this operation. Fun isn't my job."

Fred rolled his eyes. "Oh, pardon me, Your Majesty. How *could* I forget? You're the star of the show."

"I am!" Peanut chirped, puffing up his chest. "You've seen the comments online. People love me."

"They love me too." Fred smirked. "I'm the funny one."

"You're the messy one."

Their playful bickering drew a laugh from Squirrel Daddy, Mark who walked into the room holding a clipboard. He reached out to scratch Peanut behind the ears, and the squirrel leaned into the touch with a contented chirp.

"You know," the father figure said, glancing at the clipboard, "we've had more donations come in this month than ever before. And it's all thanks to you, Peanut."

Fred snorted. "Oh, sure. Let's not forget who's breaking into peanut butter jars for all those viral videos."

"You're both stars," the man said with a grin. He leaned against the couch, glancing out the window at the bright blue sky. "We're making a difference, you know. Every dollar we raise helps us save more animals. You two... you're the reason this sanctuary is still standing."

Peanut tilted his head, his eyes warm with pride. This house wasn't just a home. It was a haven. A place where animals who had nowhere else to go—animals like him and Fred—could feel safe, loved, and free.

It wasn't perfect, of course. There were always challenges. But together, they had built something worth fighting for.

Chapter 2:
The Raid

It started as a noise in the driveway.

Peanut's ears twitched at the sound of tires crunching on gravel. Fred looked up from his peanut butter, licking his paw thoughtfully.

"Are you expecting company?" Fred asked, glancing at Squirrel Mother..

She frowned, wiping her hands on a towel. "Not today."

Mark walked to the window, his eyes couldn't believe what he saw as he peered through the curtains. "That's… a lot of vehicles."

3

The sound grew louder, engines rumbling as five black SUVs rolled into the yard. Uniformed men spilled out, some holding papers, others clutching nets and cages.

The wife's face paled. "Oh no," she whispered in German, her native language.

"Stay here," Mark said, his voice tight. He opened the door and stepped outside, his hands raised. "Can I help you?"

"Department of Environmental Conservation," one of the officers barked, shoving a clipboard into his hands. "We've received a complaint about unlicensed wildlife possession."

Mark blinked, his confusion quickly turning to anger. "What? That's not possible. We're licensed for every single animal here and I'm processing a license for our pet squirrel and raccoon inside. As ridiculous as that may sound but it's your goofy idiotic rules. You can't just—"

"Step aside," the officer snapped. "We have the authority to seize any animals in violation of state law."

The wife came to the door, her voice trembling. "Please, these animals aren't just pets. They're rescues. Most of them wouldn't survive without us."

Mark frowned, his confusion quickly turning to anger. "Complaints? From who? We're licensed for every animal here. We've been running this sanctuary for years."

The officer didn't respond. He handed the clipboard to Mark, who scanned the document with growing disbelief.

"This is ridiculous," Mark said, pushing the paper back. "Every single animal here is accounted for. You can't just show up and—"

"We can and we will," the officer interrupted, gesturing for his team to move in.

"Wait!" Mark's wife stepped forward, her voice trembling. "You can't come into our home. These animals are rescues—they need us to survive!"

Mark and her plea fell on deaf ears. The officers stormed past them, spilling into the house with heavy boots and loud voices.

Peanut darted to the edge of the couch, his tiny claws digging into the fabric. Fred scrambled up beside him, his fur stood upright in terror and fear.

"What's going on?" Fred hissed.

"I don't know," Peanut whispered, his tail flicking anxiously.

The house erupted into chaos. Crates were overturned. Cabinets were yanked open. A deer in the backyard cried out as a net was thrown over her, her hooves kicking against the ground.

Two officers entered the living room, Their eyes scanned the room, landing on the couch where Peanut and Fred huddled together. "These two," one of them said, pointing. "Bag them."

Peanut's claws scraped against the fabric as gloved hands reached for him. Fred bared his teeth, but it was no use. "Run!" Fred shouted, shoving Peanut toward the edge of the couch.

But there was nowhere to go.

Peanut froze. For a moment, the world seemed to tilt beneath him.

Gloved hands grabbed them both, holding them tight despite their frantic struggles. Peanut's tiny claws scraped against the air, his heart hammering as he was thrown into a small, cold bare metal cage along with Fred, their protests muffled by the snap of the locks.

"Stop!" the wife screamed, tears streaming down her face as she reached for them. "You can't take them!" Mark tried to intervene, stepping between the officers and his animals. But he was pushed back.

Fred pressed himself against the bars, his voice shaking. "Peanut…"

Peanut said nothing. For the first time in his life, he didn't know what to say.

The officer turned his attention to her.. "Mrs.Claudia, correct?"

"Yes," she said, her accent more pronounced now. "My husband and I run this sanctuary together."

The officer smirked, his gaze flicking to the paper in his hand. "Funny, your visa says you're here on a temporary basis. Does the government know you're running a business?"

Her breath caught, her knuckles whitening as she gripped Mark's arm. "I'm not running a business. This is a non-profit. And my visa is valid and I'm married." What are you talking about?

The officer raised an eyebrow. "We'll see about that. You'll need to provide proof."

"Proof?" Mark snapped, stepping protectively in front of her. "You can't be serious. You're here about the animals, not her visa. She's done nothing wrong, she is my wife."

"Sir, I suggest you step back," the officer said coldly. "We're conducting an investigation."

"An investigation into what?" Mark's voice rose, his frustration boiling over. "We're rescuing animals! Meanwhile, in New York City, millions of people are living here illegally, beating up policemen doing their jobs and you're harassing my wife over a technicality, a visa? What kind of justice is that?"

The officer's jaw tightened. "Sir, if you interfere, we'll have no choice but to detain you both."

Mark's wife gripped his arm tightly, her eyes welling with tears. "Mark, please," she whispered. "Let's just… let's just cooperate."

Chapter 3:
Inside the House

The raid tore through the sanctuary like a wildfire.

Officers swarmed the property, their heavy boots trampling flower beds outside and kicking up dirt. Inside the house, crates were overturned, cabinets were flung open, and terrified animals were dragged from their enclosures with Peanut and Fred getting the exact opposite treatment. They were tossed into a dark empty cage like a couple of rag dolls.

"What are they doing?" Peanut whispered, his voice barely audible over the noise.

Fred's eyes darted around the room, his usual boldness gone. "It's a raid," he said, his voice low. "I've seen this before. They're here to take us away."

Peanut's heart pounded in his chest. "But why? We haven't done anything wrong!"

Fred didn't answer. He didn't have to.

The door to the living room burst open, and two officers stepped inside.

"No!" Mark's wife appeared in the doorway, her face flushed with anger. "You can't take them! They're part of our family!"

"Step aside, ma'am," the officer said, his tone cold and heartless..

Mark pushed past her, his fists clenched at his sides. "You're not taking them."

The officer reached for his belt, where a pair of handcuffs gleamed. "If you interfere, you'll be arrested for obstruction."

"No!" Mark shouted, his voice breaking as the officers forced them out the door.

"They'll be euthanized," his wife cried, clutching his arm. "Mark, they'll kill them!"

Her words hung in the air, heavy and suffocating, as the sound of engines roared to life outside.

.The house that once felt like a sanctuary now resembled a swat crime scene.

Shouts echoed through the halls as officers tore through the home, ripping open cabinets, tossing aside bedding, and upending furniture as though hunting for contraband. Peanut and Fred's cages had been shoved against the wall, their metal bars cold and unfamiliar.

Fred paced back and forth in his cage, his claws clicking against the floor. "Five hours," he muttered, his voice low and sharp. "They've been at this for five hours. What do they think they're gonna find? A stash of illegal sunflower seeds?"

Peanut didn't answer. He was huddled in the corner of his cage, his tail curled tightly around his body. His eyes darted from officer to officer as they stormed through the living room, trampling the familiar rug he and Fred used to play tag on.

"This can't be happening," Peanut whispered, his voice barely audible.

Fred paused, his ears flicking toward the front door, where Mark and his wife sat on the ground under the unrelenting heat of the afternoon sun. Two officers stood over them, arms crossed, their expressions impassive.

"Why aren't they stopping this?" Fred growled, pressing his nose against the bars. "Why aren't they fighting back?"

"Because they can't," Peanut said softly. His voice broke. "They don't have a choice."

Outside the House

Mark shifted uncomfortably on the gravel driveway, his wrists red from where the officer had shoved him to the ground earlier. His wife sat beside him, silent tears streaming down her face.

"Can I at least get some water for the animals in the backyard?" she asked, her voice hoarse. "Some of them need feeding every few hours—"

"No," one of the officers snapped, not even looking at her.

Mark's jaw tightened, his fists balling tightly in his lap. "What you're doing is illegal," he said, his voice shaking with restrained fury. "Every single animal here is registered. We've followed every law, every regulation. You have no right—"

9

"Sir," the officer interrupted, his tone dripping with indifference. "You're already under investigation for illegal wildlife possession. I'd suggest you stop making accusations."

Mark barked out a bitter laugh. "Investigation? You've already made up your mind. You're treating us like criminals because someone filed an anonymous complaint? Do you have any idea what we've done for this community? How many animals have we saved?"

"Don't make this harder on yourself," the officer said, his voice flat.

The wife sniffled quietly beside him, her shoulders trembling. Mark wrapped an arm around her, his anger simmering beneath the surface. "This is insane," he muttered under his breath. "They're acting like we're some kind of terrorists."

Chapter 4:
Passing the Torch

Peanut pressed himself against the bars of the cage, his tiny body trembling as the house—the only home he'd ever known—disappeared behind him.

The sanctuary and forest were never the same after that day.

The sanctuary, once a beacon of hope nestled between the trees, now stood empty and silent. The windows that had once glowed with warm lamplight were dark, and the soft hum of voices and laughter had been replaced by an eerie stillness. Even the birds had stopped singing.

For years, the animals of the forest had watched the sanctuary with admiration—and, if they were honest, a bit of envy. They had seen the way Peanut and Fred darted around the humans' home, safe and loved, their lives full of adventure and purpose. Peanut, with his quick wit and boundless energy, was a legend among squirrels, the kind of hero Shrimp, a neighboring noble descendant of the Peanut kind in the forest, had always dreamed of being like, his super hero Peanut. And Fred, with his clever tricks and easy charm, had made even the grumpiest raccoons puff out their chests with pride.

Now they are gone.

Word of the raid spread like wildfire throughout the forest, carried by the wind and whispered from tree to tree. The humans—*their* humans, the ones who had always been kind—had been treated like criminals. And Peanut and Fred, the heroes of the sanctuary, had been hauled away like common pests, shoved into cages and stripped of their dignity.

And then came the news no one wanted to hear: Peanut and Fred were dead, they were forcibly put to death, murdered.

The forest was thrown into mourning.

Little Shrimp crouched on a low branch, his tail curled tightly around him as he stared at the empty house in the distance. It felt wrong, seeing it so quiet. Even the Swaying Tree, where Peanut had built his famous acorn tower once when he would sneak out on rare occasions to meet and greet his fam in the forests. It looked smaller somehow, its branches drooping under the weight of silence.

"They didn't deserve this," Shrimp said softly, his voice barely carrying above the rustle of leaves.

Beside him, Lucy let out a bitter laugh. "Who deserves this?"

Shrimp turned to her, his eyes squinting. "I'm serious, Lucy. Peanut and Fred were… they were heroes. They made this place better for everyone—animals and humans. And now they're gone because of something they didn't even do."

Lucy, Shrimps partner in crime, a youngster in her own right, a doe, so called in the Raccoon kingdom, leaned back against the trunk, her sharp eyes scanning the clearing. "Yeah, well, life's not fair, Shrimp. You think those government thugs care about what's fair? They care about power. Peanut and Fred… they got caught in the middle of something bigger than them. And now they're gone."

Shrimp frowned, his claws digging into the bark beneath him. "But that's not right. They wouldn't have just given up. If it had been someone else—another squirrel, another raccoon—they would've done something to help."

Lucy raised an eyebrow. "What are you saying?"

Shrimp straightened, his tail flicking with determination. "I'm saying someone has to take up their torch. Someone has to finish what they started."

Lucy stared at him for a long moment, her expression unreadable. Finally, she sighed, pushing herself to her feet. "You've got acorn crumbs for brains, you know that?"

Shrimp blinked, taken aback. "What's that supposed to mean?"

"It means you're crazy," Lucy said, hopping onto a higher branch. "But if you're serious about this, then you're gonna need help. And lucky for you, I've got nothing better to do."

A slow grin spread across little Shrimp's cute face. "Really?"

"Don't make me regret this," Lucy muttered, leaping to another branch. "Now come on. We've got work to do."

Chapter 5:
The Memorial Service

The forest animals gathered in the clearing that night, their shadows long under the pale light of the full moon. They stood in a solemn circle around the Swaying Tree, their heads bowed and their voices hushed.

At the center of the circle, a small pile of offerings lay beneath the tree: shiny stones and feathers, acorns and berries, bits of ribbon and string. They were gifts for Peanut and Fred, tokens of gratitude from the animals who had admired them from afar.

Bram the Owl, the oldest and wisest creature in the forest, perched on a low branch, his feathers ruffled with sorrow. "Tonight," he began, his voice deep and resonant, "we honor two of our own. Peanut the Squirrel and Fred the Raccoon were more than just animals. They were symbols of hope, of kindness, of everything this forest stands for."

The animals murmured in agreement, their voices thick with emotion.

"They may be gone," Bram continued, "but their legacy lives on. It is up to us to carry their torch, to continue their work, to ensure that their sacrifice was not in vain."

Shrimp stepped forward, his small frame trembling but his voice steady. "Peanut believed in helping others. He believed that even the smallest of us could make a difference. I… I want to be like him. I want to make this forest a better place."

Lucy rolled her eyes from her spot in the back, but there was a flicker of pride in her gaze as she watched Shrimp.

Bram tilted his head, his sharp eyes studying the young squirrel. "And what about you, Lucy?" he asked. "You were Fred's kin, were you not?" Lucy a young Doe, young lady Raccoon.

Lucy hesitated, her tail twitching nervously. "Fred was my grandfather," she said finally, her voice quieter than usual. "He taught me everything I know about surviving. But Peanut and Fred… they were about more than just survivors, weren't they?" She took a deep breath, meeting Bram's gaze. "I'll help. Someone's gotta keep little Shrimp out of trouble."

A ripple of quiet laughter spread through the crowd, easing the tension.

Bram nodded solemnly. "Very well. The two of you will lead this effort. Together, we will ensure that Peanut and Fred's legacy lives on. We will protect this forest, and we will honor their memory."

Chapter 6:
The Forest Awakens

The mood shifted after the memorial. What had begun as a quiet night of mourning turned into something else—a call to action. The animals began to whisper among themselves, exchanging ideas and forming plans.

"We'll need to gather supplies," a rabbit said.

"And keep watch for the humans," added a fox.

"We can use the tunnels under the clearing," said a mole. "They'll make a good hiding spot."

Shrimp and Lucy stood at the center of it all, their heads spinning as the animals around them began to organize.

"Well," Lucy said, nudging Shrimp with her elbow. "You wanted to take up the torch. Better get ready to run with it."

Shrimp swallowed hard but nodded. For the first time since the raid, he felt a spark of hope. Peanut and Fred were gone, but their work wasn't finished. And he was ready to do whatever it took to make them proud.

The sanctuary had been quiet for weeks.

Too quiet.

The once-bustling yard, where animals roamed freely under the watchful care of Mark and his wife, now felt eerily still. The deer pen was empty. The aviary stood silent. The only sounds came from the occasional shuffle of horses in the paddock and the quiet sighs of Mark and his wife as they tended to the remaining rescues that the raid hadn't taken.

A Spark of Hope

The first light of dawn spilled over the horizon, casting long shadows across the yard. The sanctuary had been quiet for weeks—too quiet. Mark's once steady voice, calling for Peanut or Fred, was silent. The clatter of bowls, the soft murmur of his wife tending to the rescues, all of it had become subdued, weighed down by the loss of the animals who had brought the sanctuary to life.

"They look so sad," Shrimp whispered, tilting his head.

From their perch in the Swaying Tree, Shrimp and Lucy watched the humans in the yard. Mark moved slowly, his shoulders slumped as he shoveled hay into the horse trough. His wife Claudia brushed the mane of one of the horses, her movements mechanical and detached.

"They look awful," Shrimp whispered, his tail twitching. Lucy leaned back against the trunk, her arms crossed. "Yeah, well, that's what happens when your whole life gets turned upside down."

Shrimp frowned, his claws digging into the bark beneath him. He couldn't stand it—seeing the humans like this. These were the same people who had saved countless animals, who had turned their home into a haven for those in need. They didn't deserve this.

"They're hurting," Little Shrimp said softly.

Lucy leaned against the branch beside him, one paw lazily hanging down. "Yeah, well, what did you expect? They just lost Peanut and my grandpa, Freddy the freeloader. Pretty sure those two were the only reason they didn't go whacko running this place."

Shrimp frowned, his claws digging into the bark. "They need something."

Lucy raised an eyebrow. "What, like a hug? Hate to break it to you, Shrimp, but we're not exactly big enough for that."

"No, not a hug. Something... Peanut-y," Shrimp said, his eyes focusing as an idea began to take shape. "Something to remind them that not all hope is lost. That the forest is still here for them."

Lucy blinked. "Oh no. You've got that look in your eye."

"What look?"

"The one Peanut used to get right before he did something crazy."

Shrimp grinned. "Good. That means I'm on the right track."

Down in the Yard

Mark sighed as he leaned against the fence, watching the horses lazily chew on their morning hay. The mare closest to him, a chestnut rescue named Ginger, snorted softly, nudging his hand with her nose.

"I know, girl," he murmured, stroking her neck. "It's too quiet, isn't it? I miss them too."

Behind him, Claudia set down her brush and glanced toward the barn. "Do you think we'll ever feel... normal again?" she asked quietly.

Mark didn't answer right away. He stared at the house in the distance, the memories of Peanut and Fred playing in the living room flashing through his mind. "I don't know," he said finally. "Maybe."

The sound of rustling leaves drew their attention toward the forest edge. Mark straightened, his brow furrowing as he scanned the treeline.

"What is it?" his wife asked, stepping closer.

"I'm not sure," Mark said. "Thought I saw something move."

And then, without warning, chaos erupted.

Chapter 7:
Shrimp's Peanut-Inspired Prank

Shrimp moved like a shadow, hugging the edges of the yard as he made his way toward the porch. He paused behind a flower pot, his nose twitching as he made sure the coast was clear. Mark and his wife were still occupied, their gazes distant, their movements slow.

With a burst of speed, Shrimp dashed up the porch steps, grabbed the bag of peanuts in his teeth, and disappeared back into the forest before anyone could notice.

Lucy was waiting for him on the branch, one eyebrow raised. "And what, exactly, are you planning to do with that?"

Shrimp dropped the bag at her feet, his tail flicking with excitement. "You'll see."

A few minutes later, Mark straightened from where he'd been leaning against the fence. His wife had finished weeding the garden and stood, wiping her hands on her jeans.

"Do you want to check on the horses before lunch?" she asked softly.

Mark nodded, but before he could reply, something small and fast zipped past the corner of his vision. He turned his head, his face in shock..

"What was that?"

His wife frowned, following his gaze. "What was what?"

Before he could answer, another blur of movement caught his attention. This time, he saw it clearly: a peanut, bouncing across the yard like it had a mind of its own.

Mark blinked. "Was that… a peanut?"

His wife tilted her head, confused. "A peanut?"

As if in response, another peanut shot out from behind the barn, arcing high into the air before landing neatly in the horse trough. The chestnut mare sniffed at it curiously, then tossed her head as though amused.

Mark's wife's lips twitched. "What in the world…"

And then they saw it.

From the edge of the garden, Shrimp emerged, dragging a string of peanuts tied together. He zigzagged across the yard, the line of nuts bouncing behind him as though he were leading a parade.

Mark let out a startled laugh. "Is that—?"

But before he could finish the sentence, Lucy appeared, perched on the porch rail with the bag of peanuts in her paws. She tipped the bag just slightly, letting a handful of nuts cascade onto the ground. Then, with a dramatic flick of her tail, she launched herself onto the fence, where she balanced on her hind legs like a tightrope walker.

The couple watched, frozen in disbelief, as Shrimp and Lucy worked together to stage their absurd little production. Shrimp darted around the yard, hiding peanuts in the flower pots, the garden bed, and even Mark's boots. Lucy, meanwhile, climbed the fence posts, her movements theatrical as she dropped peanuts like confetti.

Mark's wife clapped a hand over her mouth, but a laugh escaped anyway—a short, sharp sound that quickly turned into a full-bodied giggle.

Mark stared at her for a moment, his eyes wide, and then he started laughing too.

The Aftermath

When the peanuts were gone and the parade was over, Shrimp and Lucy retreated to the treetops, watching from the shadows as the couple stood together in the yard, their laughter still echoing softly in the air.

"They're smiling," Shrimp whispered, his chest swelling with pride.

Lucy rolled her eyes, but there was a hint of a smile tugging at the corners of her mouth. "Yeah, well, don't let it go to your head."

Shrimp leaned back against the branch, letting out a contented sigh. For the first time in weeks, the sanctuary didn't feel so heavy. The humans were laughing again, and maybe—just maybe—that was enough.

The First Step

The next morning, Mark found a peanut on the porch.

It was perfectly placed, sitting upright on the top step as though it had been left there on purpose. He picked it up, a small smile tugging at his lips.

"Guess we've got new neighbors," he said to Claudia as she joined him.

She looked at the peanut, then out toward the forest. For a moment, she didn't say anything. But then she smiled too, small and quiet but real.

"Maybe we should leave something for them," she said finally.

Mark glanced at her, his smile widening. "Like what?"

She shrugged. "I don't know. Something that says... welcome."

Mark set the peanut down on the porch railing, his gaze drifting toward the trees. He didn't see anything—just shadows and sunlight filtering through the branches—but he felt something.

HOPE.

Chapter 8:

The New Neighbors

The days had grown a little brighter at the sanctuary.

Mark noticed it in small ways. The heaviness that had pressed down on the yard since the raid wasn't gone, but it had begun to lift. His wife was laughing more, even if only in quick bursts when she caught sight of something silly—like the way one of the rescue goats kept stealing hay from the horses, or the way a blue jay insisted on perching on her shoulder as she worked in the garden.

And there was something else. A feeling. A presence.

It started with the peanut.

Mark had found it early one morning, balanced perfectly on the porch railing. He had stared at it for a long time, his fingers brushing over its smooth surface as a faint smile crept across his face. He didn't need to see who had left it to know.

"Peanut would've done something like this," he'd murmured to himself, turning the little nut over in his hand.

That day, he decided to leave something in return.

Testing the Waters

Mark stepped onto the porch, carrying a small tin in his hands. Inside were sunflower seeds, some apple slices, and a handful of peanut but-

25

ter crackers. He placed the tin carefully on the railing, brushing a few crumbs off the wood.

"That should do it," he said, glancing over his shoulder at his Claudia.

She stood in the doorway, a kitchen towel draped over her shoulder. "You really think they'll come back?"

Mark smiled faintly. "They've been watching us. I can feel it."

She tilted her head, her lips twitching into a small smile. "Well, if they're anything like Peanut and Fred, they won't be able to resist peanut butter crackers."

Mark chuckled softly. "Let's hope so."

They stepped back inside, leaving the tin on the railing. But they didn't go far—just behind the curtain of the living room window, where they could watch the porch without being seen.

Shrimp and Lucy's Approach

From the edge of the forest, Shrimp's nose twitched. He sat crouched in the tall grass, his sharp eyes locked on the tin.

"Do you see that?" he whispered.

Beside him, Lucy leaned against a tree, her arms crossed. "Yeah, I see it."

"They left it for us," Shrimp said, his tail flicking with excitement.

Lucy raised an eyebrow. "And you're sure it's not a trap?"

Shrimp rolled his eyes. "Why would they trap us? They're the kind humans, remember? Peanut and Fred trusted them."

Lucy huffed. "Yeah, and look how that turned out."

Shrimp hesitated, his claws digging into the dirt. "It's different now," he said softly. "Peanut and Fred... they didn't deserve what happened to them. But Mark and his wife didn't do it. They loved them."

Lucy glanced at him, her expression softening just slightly. "You really think they want us around?"

Shrimp nodded. "I do."

Lucy sighed, her tail twitching. "Fine. But if this goes sideways, I'm blaming you."

Shrimp grinned. "Deal."

He darted out of the grass, moving quickly but cautiously as he approached the porch. Lucy followed at a slower pace, her sharp eyes scanning for any sign of danger.

When they reached the tin, Shrimp climbed onto the railing, sniffing curiously at the contents. The scent of peanut butter made his nose twitch with delight.

Lucy hopped onto the porch, sitting on her haunches as she inspected the tin. "Well," she said, "at least they've got good taste."

Shrimp reached into the tin and grabbed a cracker, nibbling it eagerly. He turned toward the window, his sharp eyes catching a faint movement behind the curtain. For a moment, he froze, his tiny heart thudding in his chest.

And then he saw them.

Mark and Claudia were watching from the window, their faces partially obscured by the curtain. They weren't moving, just standing there quietly, their eyes full of something that Shrimp couldn't quite name.

Shrimp raised the cracker in his tiny paw, holding it up as if in thanks.

Behind the curtain, Mark smiled.

The Connection

It became a routine after that.

Every morning, Mark or Claudia would leave something on the porch: a handful of peanuts, a few slices of apple, sometimes even a bit of leftover bread or cheese. And every day, Shrimp and Lucy would appear, cautiously at first, but with growing confidence as the days went by.

Shrimp always ate first, his enthusiasm uncontainable as he darted back and forth between the tin and the porch railing. Lucy, on the other hand, took her time. She would sniff the offerings carefully, watching the house with wary eyes before finally helping herself.

Mark and his wife began spending more time on the porch, sitting quietly with their tea as the two animals scurried around them. They didn't try to approach, didn't make any sudden movements— just sat and watched, their presence calm and steady.

It was on one of these mornings, as Shrimp perched on the railing nibbling on a peanut, that Mark spoke for the first time.

"You remind me of someone," he said softly, his voice carrying just enough to reach Shrimps' little ears.

Shrimp paused, his tiny paws gripping the peanut as he tilted his head.

Mark smiled, his eyes warm. "He was small like you. Fast, too. And clever. Always getting into trouble."

Shrimp blinked, his tail flicking slightly.

Lucy, who was lounging near the porch steps, let out a quiet huff. "Oh, great," she muttered under her breath. "Now they're talking to us."

But she didn't leave.

A Happy Beginning

By the end of the week, Shrimp and Lucy had become regular visitors. They didn't come every hour of the day—not yet—but they came often enough that the sanctuary started to feel a little less empty.

Mark and Claudia still missed Peanut and Fred. That much would never change. But as they watched Shrimp tumble off the railing in an overzealous attempt to grab a cracker, or Lucy scowl at him from her spot on the porch steps, they began to feel something they hadn't felt in a long time.

A future.

Chapter 9:
A New Day at the Ranch

The morning sun bathed the sanctuary in soft, golden light. For the first time in weeks, the air felt lighter—less like it was clinging to the grief that had settled over the yard and more like it was moving, flowing again.

Mark stood on the porch, a steaming cup of coffee cradled in his hands. He stared out at the yard, watching as the light crept across the fence posts and the barn roof, the shadows retreating into the forest. It wasn't the same, and maybe it never would be. But something about this morning felt... different.

"Good morning," his wife said, stepping out onto the porch beside him.

Mark said. "Couldn't sleep. Just wanted to... I don't know. Check on things."

She nodded, leaning against the porch railing. For a while, they stood in comfortable silence, sipping their drinks and letting the sounds of the sanctuary wash over them—the rustle of leaves in the breeze, the soft nickering of the horses, the distant call of a blue jay.

And then Mark spotted it.

"There," he said softly, nudging his wife's arm.

She followed his gaze to the bottom step of the porch. Sitting in the same spot as the day before was another peanut. This one had been carefully placed on its side, as if it had been posed for a picture.

Her lips curved into a faint smile. "It's them, isn't it? The squirrel and the raccoon."

Mark chuckled, shaking his head. "I think so. They're bold, I'll give them that."

"Do you think they're... leaving us gifts?" she asked, tilting her head.

Mark leaned forward, inspecting the peanut. "Maybe. Or maybe they're just trying to get more snacks."

She laughed softly. "Well, either way, we should leave something for them."

Mark raised an eyebrow. "You want to encourage them?"

"They're trying to say something," she said simply. "Maybe we should say something back."

Mark considered this for a moment, then nodded. "All right. But let's make it something good."

The Offering

Later that afternoon, Mark carried a small wooden bowl out to the porch. Inside was a handful of sunflower seeds, a few chunks of apple, and a single, perfect peanut.

He set the bowl on the top step, then stepped back, retreating to the swing at the far end of the porch where his wife was waiting.

"You think they'll come?" she asked, watching as Mark settled in beside her.

"They're squirrels and raccoons," Mark said with a small grin. "If they don't show up for food, I'll be shocked."

The Encounter

Mark and his wife sat quietly on the porch swing, their movements slow and measured as they watched the yard.

It started as a rustle in the grass—soft, almost imperceptible. Then a flash of gray darted across the clearing, pausing near the base of the porch steps.

"It's him," Mark murmured, his voice barely above a whisper.

Shrimp crouched at the bottom of the steps, his nose twitching as he eyed the bowl. He took one cautious step forward, then another, his tiny claws clicking softly against the wood.

Mark's wife held her breath as the squirrel reached the top step and leaned over the bowl, sniffing the contents.

And then, just as little Shrimp grabbed a sunflower seed, Lucy appeared. She moved with far less subtlety, hopping onto the porch with a loud *thump* that made Mark laugh softly.

The raccoon stared at the humans for a long moment, her eyes sharp and calculating. Then, without breaking eye contact, she reached into the bowl, grabbed the peanut, and scurried back to the yard.

Shrimp hesitated for a moment, glancing between the humans and the bowl. Then he grabbed a chunk of apple, gave the humans a quick nod, and followed Lucy back into the trees.

Mark leaned back in the swing, a slow smile spreading across his face. "Well, that was something."

His wife chuckled, resting her head on his shoulder. "You think they'll come back?"

Mark's gaze lingered on the edge of the forest. "I hope so."

In the Forest

Back in the safety of the trees, Shrimp perched on a low branch, nibbling at the apple chunk. Lucy sat nearby, holding the peanut between her paws as she eyed it suspiciously.

"Well?" Shrimp asked, tilting his head.

"Well what?" Lucy replied.

"What do you think? They left us food."

Lucy shrugged. "It's food. It's not a promise."

For the first time since Peanut and Fred had been taken, things felt… okay. Not perfect, not fixed, but okay.

And maybe that was enough.

Shrimp frowned, but he didn't argue. Deep down, he knew Lucy was still guarded—still hesitant to trust after everything that had happened to Peanut and Fred. But he couldn't shake the feeling that this was different.

Chapter 10:
The Torch Burns Bright

The sun was low in the sky, its golden rays painting the sanctuary yard in warm hues. Mark stood on the porch, watching as Shrimp scampered across the grass, a peanut clenched triumphantly in his tiny teeth.

"Look at him go," Mark said with a chuckle, shaking his head. "I swear, he's got the same spark Peanut used to have."

His wife leaned against the railing, a soft smile tugging at her lips. "And Lucy's got Fred's attitude. Did you see her this morning? She was sitting on the fence like she owned the place."

Mark nodded, his gaze drifting to the edge of the forest. The shadows were longer now, stretching toward the sanctuary like an invitation. For weeks, it had felt like the forest was pulling away, retreating into itself in the wake of Peanut and Fred's loss. But now, it felt different—like it was leaning in, reaching out.

Shrimp darted up the porch steps and dropped the peanut at Mark's feet, his tiny chest puffed out like he'd just completed the most daring heist in history. Mark laughed, bending down to pick it up.

"Thanks, buddy," he said, holding the peanut up like it was a trophy.

Shrimp chirped in response, his tail flicking wildly. He raced back down the steps, pausing halfway to glance over his shoulder.

"Does he want us to follow him?" Mark's wife asked, raising an eyebrow.

Mark shrugged. "Only one way to find out."

They followed Shrimp across the yard, their footsteps soft against the grass. Lucy joined them halfway, her movements slower and more deliberate, but there was a glimmer of curiosity in her sharp eyes.

Shrimp led them to the Swaying Tree, its massive branches casting long shadows over the clearing. At the base of the tree, a group of forest animals had gathered—rabbits, foxes, birds, even a few deer. They parted slightly as Shrimp approached, creating a small path that led to the heart of the circle.

Mark and his wife stopped at the edge of the gathering, their breath catching as they saw what lay at the center.

It was a small pile of offerings: acorns, feathers, shiny stones, bits of ribbon, and a few pieces of fruit. Nestled among the items were two carvings etched into the base of the tree—a squirrel and a raccoon, their figures simple but unmistakable.

Mark felt a lump rise in his throat. "Peanut and Fred," he whispered.

His wife reached for his hand, her fingers curling around his. "They've made a memorial," she said softly.

Shrimp and Lucy stood at the base of the tree, side by side. The little squirrel glanced up at the humans, his wide eyes sparkling with something that looked almost like pride. Lucy rolled her eyes but gave a small, reluctant nod, as if to say, "Yeah, we helped."

Mark knelt, brushing his fingers against the carvings. For a moment, he didn't say anything. The weight of everything they'd lost—and everything they'd gained—hung in the air like a quiet prayer.

Finally, he looked up at Shrimp and Lucy, his eyes warm. "Thank you," he said simply.

Shrimp chirped in response, leaping onto Lucy's back in an impromptu victory pose. The raccoon let out a dramatic sigh but didn't push him off, her tail flicking as she turned to face the crowd of forest animals.

Mark and his wife stepped back, giving the animals their space as the forest came alive with quiet murmurs and rustling leaves. It wasn't just a memorial—it was a promise. A vow to protect the sanctuary, the forest, and everything Peanut and Fred had fought for.

The Next Morning

Mark stepped onto the porch, a steaming cup of coffee in his hands. The yard was quiet, but it was a good kind of quiet—the kind that buzzed with potential.

At the edge of the porch, a small pile of peanuts sat neatly stacked, each one carefully arranged like a gift. Mark chuckled, shaking his head.

"They've got big shoes to fill," his wife said, stepping out behind him.

Mark smiled. "They're doing just fine."

In the distance, Shrimp and Lucy darted between the trees, their movements quick and chaotic. They didn't need to be Peanut and Fred. They just needed to be themselves.

And as Mark watched them disappear into the forest, he felt something he hadn't felt in a long time.

The memory of Peanut and Fred would live forever.

The End